2/4/25

To Fr. Gabe

thank you for your service
to the Church. Hope you
get into ALL your Ph.D.

programs!

Best wishes,
Christopher

Praying Like Saint Augustine

PRAYING
LIKE
SAINT
AUGUSTINE

A GUIDED
PRAYER JOURNAL

CHRISTOPHER KACZOR

Our Sunday Visitor
Huntington, Indiana

Nihil Obstat
Msgr. Michael Heintz, Ph.D.
Censor Librorum

Imprimatur
✠ Kevin C. Rhoades
Bishop of Fort Wayne-South Bend
March 7, 2024

The *Nihil Obstat* and *Imprimatur* are official declarations that a book is free from doctrinal or moral error. It is not implied that those who have granted the *Nihil Obstat* and *Imprimatur* agree with the contents, opinions, or statements expressed.

Our Sunday Visitor Publishing Division
Our Sunday Visitor, Inc.
200 Noll Plaza
Huntington, IN 46750
www.osv.com
1-800-348-2440

ISBN: 978-1-63966-147-3 (Inventory No. T2858)
1. RELIGION / Christian Living / Devotional Journal
2. RELIGION / Christian Living / Prayer
3. RELIGION / Christianity / Catholic
eISBN: 978-1-63966-148-0

Cover design: Tyler Ottinger
Cover art: AdobeStock
Interior design: Amanda Falk
Interior art: AdobeStock

PRINTED IN THE UNITED STATES OF AMERICA

Dedicated to Elizabeth, Tucker, and Arthur,
in thanksgiving for bringing such great joy to our whole family

Contents

Introduction

Saint Augustine wrote many famous works, but the most famous of all is his *Confessions*. In this autobiography, Augustine explores his early life, his wandering far from God, and his journey back to God facilitated by two saints, his mother, Monica, and the bishop Ambrose of Milan. But his *Confessions* is not written to his mother or to Ambrose or to any human reader. In his *Confessions*, St. Augustine of Hippo wrote to God. "Allow me to speak," Augustine wrote, "for I am addressing your Mercy, not a man who would laugh at me." Although the *Confessions* have been read by countless readers since they were written around AD 400, Augustine wrote to God and for God about his childhood, his gratitude to his mother, his friends, his triumphs and tragedies, and his hope for eternal life.

In prayer, I am no Saint Augustine. When I try to speak to God and listen to God, I find myself often distracted. I say something to God (either out loud or in my mind), but all too quickly I find myself thinking about yesterday's lunch, today's trouble, or tomorrow's trip. When I try to listen to God, the difficulty doubles.

Of course, these distractions can themselves become material for prayer. I can communicate with God about whatever springs to my mind: past, present, or future. But all too often prayer drifts into daydreaming. St. Teresa of Ávila imagined distractions as the "madwoman of the house," who bursts into conversations unwelcomed with irrelevant things to say. Time devoted to prayer can often become a time of the restless mind worrying, planning, and pondering, but not really praying. When I speak to God with my mouth or in my mind, I notice — often within seconds — that other things spring into focus. So, how do we fight the distractions of the madwoman or madman inside each one of us?

There is one way of praying that I found dramatically minimizes my distractions. It is the way of prayer used by Augustine in his *Confessions*. Augustine wrote to God about his own life, and this helped him see God's care for him in daily events. I have found that when I write a letter to Jesus (or God the Father, or the Holy Spirit), my mind becomes more focused on communicating with God. There is something about putting pen to paper that organizes my thoughts and protects against the inner lunatic running around in my mind, distracting me.

When I write a letter to God, and imagine what God would write back to me, I find I can stay in communication with God much more effectively. When I write, distractions still can arise, but they tend to be minimized, and my focus on communicating with God is maximized. Writing works to diminish distractions because when you put pen to paper, you need to slow down. And when you slow down, your thoughts cease whizzing past you in a swirl. Each sentence brings its own order, and a tangle of fighting tigers of thoughts, feelings, and impulses gets tamed.

As a guided prayer journal, this book is an effort to dampen distractions and facilitate praying as a real communication with God. In writing about your daily life, your history, and your hopes for the future, you'll be traveling along the path of Augustine's *Confessions*. In writing letters to God, you'll also be following in the footsteps of the great American Catholic author Flannery O'Connor, whose letters that began "Dear God" were published fifty years after her death.

For prayer to be a true two-way communication, we must not only communicate to God (with our mouths or with our pen) but also listen to God. And so, each prompt in this book includes a chance to imagine what God would say in reply to you. Each day is different, so each day has its own personalized and individualized communication to and from God (or from Mary or a saint, as you choose). I notice that my letters often begin with what I am feeling at the moment. Here is an example of what this looks like from my own life:

Dear Jesus,

I'm so irritated with Francine. She talks and talks without even pausing to listen to a word I say. It is as if she thinks I was sent by *The New York Times* to interview her. *And* she is so opinionated. She is right, and everyone who sees things differently (including, of course, me) is wrong. Period. I positively want to run away whenever I have to talk to her. When I see her in the coffee room, my need for caffeine suddenly disappears. But, of course, I cannot flee every time she's around. So please, Jesus, help me to deal with her. Let me see what is true, good, beautiful, and kind in her despite all these things being well disguised under a torrential downpour of words.

Love, Chris

Dear Chris,

Yes, Francine is certainly a talkative person. Can you remember to focus not just on what irritates you about her but on the good I've given her? She is, as you know, fantastically generous in her committee work. Do you remember how much help she gave you when you were trying to plan the going away party for your colleague?

She has her negative points, yes, but she also has much that's positive. Can you be patient, be kind, and be generous with her? Did you ever think that she talks so much because she is so lonely? If you were alone as much as she is alone, wouldn't you be dying to share what's on your mind? Yes, she is irritating sometimes, but this is a great opportunity for you to grow in kindness and patience and ability to listen well as I do for you.

Love, Jesus

When listening for what Jesus (or the Holy Spirit, or Mary) might say in reply to you, it is important to keep in mind that we can be mistaken about what we think God is saying to us. This is true even if we use the very words of Scripture. Imagine someone picks up the Bible and reads that Judas "hanged himself" (Mt 27:5) and then flipping to a different passage reads, "Go and do likewise" (Lk 10:37). How can we know if our understanding of Scripture or our imagination of what God is saying to us is mistaken? We can ask ourselves two questions when trying to determine if what we imagine God is saying to us is authentic.

1. *Is the message contrary to love of God, neighbor, and self?* In his book *On Christian Doctrine*, Saint Augustine taught that any interpretation of Scripture that undermines love of God or love of neighbor is a false interpretation of Scripture. To read Judas "hanged himself" (Mt 27:5) and "go and do likewise" (Lk 10:37) as a command from God to commit suicide is mistaken. To commit suicide undermines love of God and love of neighbor. God desires our life, not our death. And suicide undermines the human community, leaving those left behind with sadness and often guilt. So, any idea that goes against love of God, love of neighbor, or love of self is not from God.

2. *Is the message contrary to the teachings of the Catholic Church?* In his *Spiritual Exercises*, St. Ignatius of Loyola pointed out that God does not contradict himself by telling a private individual something that goes against what God teaches publicly through his Church. God's private revelations do not contradict God's public revelation. So, a married person who imagines that God is calling him to commit adultery is mistaken. Any idea that goes against what God has revealed publicly to the Church is not from God.

Whenever you imagine what God would say back to you in a letter, keep in mind these truths articulated by Saint Augustine and Saint Ignatius. What God says to us can never contradict God's nature as perfect Love and Mercy. What God says to us can never contradict what God says to everyone in public revelation as confirmed by the Church.

When in doubt, confirm with a trusted spiritual advisor. Especially about important decisions, it is wise to consult with learned, experienced, and holy people (perhaps a priest confessor) to make sure that you are not mistakenly imagining God's call. A good spiritual director can help us discern God's will in our lives. Indeed, journaling our conversations with God can also give us lots of insight into what we need to discuss with a spiritual director.

Each day of our lives brings its own joys and sufferings, its own gifts and challenges. So, each day is a chance to communicate again with Jesus (or the Father, or the Holy Spirit, or Mary or a saint as you choose) about what is on your heart and mind that day.

HOW TO USE THIS BOOK

When you write, you can communicate to the Divine Mercy even your deepest fears, your worst moments, your biggest regrets, your darkest shames. Augustine certainly did this in his *Confessions*. In this book, I encourage you to put it all out there in total honesty.

If you worry that somebody might come across what you write and you want to avoid an unwanted reader of your private communications, feel free to tear out that page. Burn it into cinders, flush it down the toilet, or rip it into a thousand pieces. Writing in this book can be your time for total transparency and humble honesty. God already knows everything. But if you write with complete candor, you might learn what you need to help you grow. You might, with God's help, get to know better the Living Light that shines in the darkness, the Kindly Light no darkness can ever overcome.

In this book, you'll find reflections from Scripture, or the writings of saints and sages, as a prompt for your letter to God and what you imagine God would write back to you. The book is divided into three parts: reflections on gratitude, reflections on suffering, and reflections on discerning God's will. All of our lives include positive elements, for which gratitude is appropriate, and negative elements, for which reflecting on suffering is appropriate. Finally, we all face uncertainties, for which reflecting on God's will for us is appropriate.

On a particular day, the first reflection you read may not be fitting for your own circumstances. If so, feel free to skip around and find a passage that fits better with your current experience. You may also find it helpful to read a letter you've written, and see whether further reflection is timely. You may notice that something that you were extremely worried about turned out, with God's help, to be just fine. If so, you might feel inspired to write a letter of gratitude to God for that positive resolution. The point is to write to God (and imagine what God would say to you) about what is relevant for your life right now in your current situation. My hope is that this prayer journal might deepen your love for God and help you to move forward in your spiritual journey.

When and where will you write your letters? I suggest writing in the morning. For most people, their focus, energy, and vigor are better in the morning than late at night. The likelihood of falling asleep is lower, since you just got up. If I try to pray at night, I begin to pray but soon am not talking to God but dozing with the sandman. Of course, if you're a night owl, maybe praying at night is the best time for you. Whatever time you choose, get a comfortable chair and maybe a cup of coffee. If you write a letter to God each day, at the same time and in the same place, the odds are that within a month you'll have a solid habit that requires little effort to keep going. You can set a fixed amount of time (start with fifteen minutes or so each day) devoted exclusively for communicating with God.

You may miss a day or a week, or even longer. But you can just keep coming back and pick up where you left off. This journal can help you to continue developing your relationship with God, and God understands when the challenges of life get in the way of what we had planned to do.

Although the prompt will often be a letter to Jesus, feel free, if the Holy Spirit moves you, to write to God the Father, or to God the Holy Spirit. You might want to write to Mary and imagine what she would write back to you. You might want to write to your favorite saint or a holy person from your past like a grandparent. Each day is a new opportunity to communicate with God or with some holy individual (Mary and the saints). You can write your letter first, and then imagine what God would write back. Or, if it seems better, you can write first what you think God would say to you, and then you can respond to that letter. Each day has its own blank space for your letter. At the back of the book are a few extra blank pages in case you wish to write more on a particular day.

This practice of writing can include making a list. There is even scientific evidence that such writing helps us. Stanford University Professor of Medicine Andrew Huberman notes, "Making this list each morning is very effective in part because it captures key elements from the science of goal seeking, emotional health and motivation." He suggests writing a list about, "1) 5 Gratitudes 2) Plans for the Day 3) Any Fears or Resentments 4) Things to Watch Out For 5) Things to Strive For." In writing a letter to God about these five things, you'll be communicating about what is currently important for you in your own circumstances.

When you write, there is no need to worry at all about your spelling and handwriting. God knows exactly what you are trying to say even if you cannot read a word of what you wrote. The worst handwriting and spelling in the world cannot prevent communication with God.

Saint Augustine wrote: "I attempt to be one of those who write because they have made some progress, and who, by means of writing, make further progress." I hope that the writing to God that you do in this book will help you make further progress into deeper love for God, for others, and for yourself. May this book be your own version of Augustine's *Confessions* written to the most important audience of all, the First Love, God All Merciful.

PART I
Thanksgiving

I give you thanks, my God, who are my sweetness, my honor, and my confidence. I give you thanks for your gifts. Preserve these gifts for me. For you will save me, and will increase and perfect the gifts you have given for me. And I will be with you, since you have given me my own existence.
CONFESSIONS, BOOK ONE

The Bible teaches us, "In all circumstances give thanks, for this is the will of God for you in Christ Jesus" (1 Thes 5:18). "O give thanks to the Lord, for he is good, / for his mercy endures forever" (Ps 136:1, RSV). To give thanks to God for his blessings is itself to receiving a blessing from God. Whenever we are grateful, we turn our eyes towards what is true, good, noble, just, pure, lovely, and gracious. Whenever we are grateful, we can have some taste of God's generosity to us.

If we take the time, we can recognize countless people — parents, teachers, coaches, friends, and family — who have given to us what we needed and what we wanted. If we take the time, we can recognize God as the ultimate first giver of all these gifts. For it is God who was the First Cause of our family and friends. God himself is the ultimate gift giver who gives to us for our own good. Augustine saw God's providential gifts working through his mother, Monica, and through the good bishop, St. Ambrose of Milan. If we are attentive, we can see the gifts of God in our own lives. And when we see these gifts, it can enable us to love God better than before.

Reflecting on the birth of Jesus and the visit of the shepherds, Mary "kept all these things, reflecting on them in her heart" (Lk 2:19). Write to God about one of your most treasured memories. What do you think God would write in reply?

After thirteen years in a communist prison, Venerable Francis Xavier Nguyên Văn Thuân, a Vietnamese cardinal, wrote, "Thank you for the people who place obstacles on my path and cause me trouble; they help me to become holy. Thank you for allowing me to live in this particular time in history. Thank you for giving me a share in your bitter chalice. How can I repay you, Lord, for filling my life with so many good things?" What people has God placed in your path who are helping you become holy? What sufferings may actually be "good things" for which you can thank God?

"The secret of happiness is to live moment by moment and to thank God for what he is sending us every day in his goodness," wrote St. Gianna Beretta Molla, a Catholic medical doctor who died to preserve the life of her youngest child in utero. What does God give you today for which you can be grateful?

Pope St. John Paul II taught, "For us, Christians, thanksgiving is expressed fully in the Eucharist. In every Holy Mass, we bless the Lord, God of the universe, presenting to him the bread and wine, the fruits 'of the earth and of the work of human hands.'" Let us thank God for the miracle at each Mass of changing the bread and wine into the great gift of his Body and Blood in holy Communion. Do you have a memory of a particular Mass that still gives you joy?

In his *Divine Comedy,* the poet Dante Alighieri called God the "First Love." How did Jesus, even before your birth, show his love for you? How can you show your love to him today?

To the Angel Gabriel, Mary said, "Behold, I am the handmaid of the Lord. May it be done to me according to your word" (Lk 1:38). In following the plan proposed by the Angel Gabriel, Mary brought Jesus to the world. Has the intercession of Mary ever brought you a gift for which you are grateful?

"All the ends of the earth have seen / the victory of our God" (Ps 98:3). Do you believe that God is truly victorious, even in your life? From what has God saved you? From what does God want to save you?

"Now there were shepherds in that region living in the fields and keeping the night watch over their flock. The angel of the Lord appeared to them and the glory of the Lord shone around them, and they were struck with great fear. The angel said to them, 'Do not be afraid; for behold, I proclaim to you good news of great joy that will be for all the people. For today in the city of David a savior has been born for you who is Messiah and Lord'" (Lk 2:8–11). Like the shepherds, perhaps you have been in great fear. Has your fear ever been turned into joy? Has something terrible in your life ever changed into something wonderful? How has God helped you grow in spite of your fears or even through your fears?

After defeating the Nazis and saving Britain in World War II, Winston Churchill lost his bid for reelection as prime minister. His wife, Clementine, tried to console him: "Winston, this could be a blessing in disguise." Churchill replied, "If this is a blessing, it is certainly very well disguised." Churchill came to recognize the wisdom of his wife's words. After he lost his election, his health improved, his writing flourished, and he won the Nobel Prize for Literature. Eventually, his political fortunes also changed for the better. Is there a blessing in your life that was originally very well disguised?

"Dear friends, may no adversity paralyze you," said Pope Benedict XVI. "Be afraid neither of the world, nor of the future, nor of your weakness. The Lord has allowed you to live in this moment of history so that, by your faith, his name will continue to resound throughout the world." What gift is the Lord giving you at this moment in history? How does he want to be glorified in this moment in history through your life?

Johann Sebastian Bach is credited with saying, "The aim and final end of all music should be none other than the glory of God and the refreshment of the soul." Write to God about the music you love most. Have you ever felt the presence of God through music?

Venerable Fulton Sheen, a twentieth-century American Catholic bishop, author, and media personality, wrote: "Years ago, we used to think of the heavens as 'way up there.' Then one day the God of the heavens came to this earth, and that hour when she held the Babe in her arms, it became true to say that with her we now 'look down' at heaven." Imagine the infant Jesus right in front of you, held in the arms of Mary after his birth. What would you say in gratitude to Mary and Jesus? How would Mary and Jesus respond?

In her Magnificat, Mary said, "From now on will all ages call me blessed" (Lk 1:48). Today, countless people all over the world will pray, "Blessed are you among women" in saying the Hail Mary. Write a gratitude letter to Mary for all she has done for you. How would the Mother of God respond?

"The lives of the saints are themselves interpretations of the Gospel," wrote twentieth-century theologian Hans Urs von Balthasar. What saint helps you most in understanding the Gospel? To which saint are you most grateful? Write to them today, expressing your gratitude. How might this saint respond?

A Gaelic proverb says, "If the best man's faults were written on his forehead, it would make him pull his hat over his eyes." We are all beggars searching for the living Bread, Jesus, the savior of us all. Thank Jesus for liberating you from your sins. Thank Jesus for giving you his Body and Blood in each Mass.

Saint Augustine said, "Whatever be our circumstances in this world, there is nothing truly enjoyable without a friend." Thank God for your friends and ask God how you might strengthen your love for them.

In a passage that is read at countless weddings, Saint Paul teaches, "Love is patient, love is kind. It is not jealous, [love] is not pompous, it is not inflated, it is not rude, it does not seek its own interests, it is not quick-tempered, it does not brood over injury, it does not rejoice over wrongdoing but rejoices with the truth" (1 Cor 13:4–8). Substitute someone's first name for the word *love* in this passage, for example, maybe your grandma or your best friend. Write to God about your gratitude for this person.

_____

_____

_____

_____

_____

_____

_____

_____

_____

_____

_____

_____

"The more we love Jesus, the more we know him, the more our true freedom develops and our joy in being redeemed flourishes. Thank you, Jesus, for your friendship!" said Pope Benedict XVI. Do you believe that Jesus desires friendship with you? Write to him about this. What does he say in reply?

In his book *The City of God*, Saint Augustine wrote about heaven, "In the everlasting City, there will remain in each and all of us an inalienable freedom of the will, emancipating us from every evil and filling us with every good, rejoicing in the inexhaustible beatitude of everlasting happiness, unclouded by the memory of any sin or sanction suffered, yet with no forgetfulness of our redemption or any loss of gratitude for our Redeemer." In Christ, we have been given the hope of heaven, the hope of becoming citizens in the everlasting City of God. How can you express your gratitude to God for offering you heavenly happiness?

"Ingratitude is the worst and most abominable of sins and in fact the origin of all sins," said St. Ignatius of Loyola, sixteenth-century Spanish priest and founder of the Society of Jesus. Where do you struggle the most to be grateful? Can you turn that into praise today, giving God thanks even if you don't feel grateful?

Catholic philosopher and author Peter Kreeft wrote, "A saint isn't somebody who tries harder, but somebody who trusts more." Is there a saint-in-training in your life that you could thank God for?

The first First Lady, Martha Washington, wrote: "I am determined to be cheerful and happy in whatever situation I may find myself. For I have learned that the greater part of our misery or unhappiness is determined not by our circumstance but by our disposition." How might God be inviting you to cultivate a disposition of cheerfulness and gratitude in your present circumstances?

"Thank you, Lord, for having chosen me to be your child. Thank you for having given me Mary for my Mother. Thank you for the mission I received from you in the Church. Thank you for having revealed your mysteries to me. Thank you for so many brothers and sisters who sustain me." Venerable Francis Xavier Cardinal Nguyên Văn Thuân wrote these words during his thirteen-year imprisonment by the Vietnamese government. Thank God for what you are grateful for today — whatever your circumstances might be.

The Anglican priest William Law wrote in his book *A Serious Call to a Devout and Holy Life*, "Whatever seeming calamity befalls you, if you can thank and praise God for it, you turn it into a blessing." Can you praise God today for a difficulty in your life? Might God be giving you a gift in this bitter medicine?

Someone once noted: "Before God brought me into existence, he saw all my faults, sins, and vices. And he brought me into existence anyway." Ask God to let you experience his divine mercy and love as you thank him for your existence.

O. Carter Snead, a legal scholar and bioethicist at Notre Dame, writes in his book *What It Means to Be Human*, "Embracing the gifts of one's life with gratitude and humility makes one especially alive to the least advantaged who have not received the gifts they need to flourish on their own." In gratitude to God, how can you offer what you have to help those in need to flourish?

Saint Paul teaches, "Whatever is true, whatever is honorable, whatever is just, whatever is pure, whatever is lovely, whatever is gracious, if there is any excellence, if there is anything worthy of praise, think about these things" (Phil 4:8) Thank God for someone in your life who is lovely, gracious, or honorable. Ask God for help in seeing what is true, honorable, just, pure, lovely, and excellent even in those you don't particularly enjoy.

"How beautiful it is to do nothing, and then rest afterward" (Spanish proverb). How can you find God in your rest? How can God find you in your rest? Have you experienced any moments of rest recently? Write about those moments and exress your gratitude to God for them.

"Let your heart overflow in effusions of Love and gratitude as you consider how God's grace each day saves you from the snares that the enemy has set in your path," wrote St. Josemaría Escrivá, a Spanish priest and founder of Opus Dei. Can you thank God today for saving you from something terrible that could have happened to you? What does God say in reply?

Chinese Cardinal Ignatius Kung spent thirty years imprisoned by the Chinese government, many of those years in solitary confinement. He wrote: "I am grateful to God for those years [in solitary], which were the greatest years of my priesthood. Because there I could imitate my Lord in His abandonment on the Cross and give my life for His people. That is where priesthood takes all its meaning." How can your own suffering help you to imitate the Lord? Write to him about it. What does Jesus say in reply?

Scripture enjoins us to give "thanks always and for everything in the name of our Lord Jesus Christ to God the Father" (Eph 5:20). What are three things that you are grateful to God for that happened yesterday? Is our Lord grateful to you for three things you did yesterday?

Thomas à Kempis, author of *The Imitation of Christ*, wrote: "He who speaks of his neighbor's virtues and good deeds places beautiful flowers before Jesus' eyes. He who devoutly reads and proclaims Jesus' words spreads fragrant aromas before his audience. He who kindly tolerates and finds excuses for another's faults will readily experience Jesus' mercy." How can you find Jesus in other people today and even in their weakness give thanks to God for their existence?

This beautiful prayer is attributed to Saint Patrick: "I arise today, through God's strength to pilot me, God's might to uphold me, God's wisdom to guide me, God's eye to look before me, God's ear to hear me, God's word to speak for me, God's hand to guard me, God's shield to protect me, God's host to save me." How can you thank God for his protection, guidance, and presence you today.

St. Catherine of Siena said, "All the way to heaven is heaven." How is Jesus giving you a foretaste of heaven even now, despite any sufferings or difficulties you may be experiencing?

The English novelist and poet Charlotte Brontë said, "Gratitude is a divine emotion: it fills the heart, but not to bursting; it warms it, but not to fever." What happened yesterday (or recently) for which you can be grateful to God?

PART II

Suffering

At this grief [the death of my friend] my heart was utterly darkened; and whatever I beheld was death. My native country was a torment to me, and my father's house a strange unhappiness; and whatever I had shared with him, wanting him, became a distracting torture. … I became a great riddle to myself, and I asked my soul, why I was so sad, and why I was so disturbed: but I did not know how to answer myself. And if I said, "Trust in God," I did not obey myself. … Only tears were sweet to me, for they followed my friend, the dearest of my affections. And now, Lord, these things are passed by, and time hath assuaged my wound.

Confessions, Book Four

In his *Confessions*, Saint Augustine describes how he suffered various difficulties and hardships, including losing a dear friend and coming close to dying himself. In these trials, he sought and he found the severe Mercy of God guiding him, helping him, and even using his suffering for his own good. Augustine knew that even the most noble and innocent people who ever existed, Jesus and his mother Mary, suffered in this life, in this valley of tears. Augustine certainly suffered, and his mother, Saint Monica, did, too. When Augustine wrote about his suffering and tried to see the hand of God even in his trials, he was able to grow. Indeed, contemporary psychological research indicates that writing about suffering can help heal that suffering. So, in these pages, you can write about your own trials, difficulties, and sufferings. You are not alone. Jesus understands your suffering, as does Mary, as do all the saints. You can, like them, make your suffering useful to yourself and to those you love. I hope these pages help you do that.

"Great crowds came to [Jesus], having with them the lame, the blind, the deformed, the mute, and many others. They placed them at his feet, and he cured them" (Mt 15:30). How are you suffering any kind of blindness or lameness or deformity, whether a physical suffering or a spiritual one? Write to Jesus about it. How do you imagine Jesus replies?

In Mark 8:2, Jesus says of those in need, "My heart is moved with pity." Ask Jesus who in your life needs God's merciful love given through you. What would Jesus say in reply?

St. Elizabeth Ann Seton, an American convert to Catholicism who was a widow, mother, religious founder, and educator, said: "We know certainly that our God calls us to a holy life. We know that he gives us every grace, every abundant grace; and though we are so weak of ourselves, this grace is able to carry us through every obstacle and difficulty." What special grace can you ask God for today? How do you imagine God responds?

"I have never yet met anyone who thought that God gave him the right cross to bear (including myself); everyone looks around with a certain wistful envy at others and says to himself, 'Now THAT is the kind of cross I could carry with equanimity, courage, even joy.' But of course what makes a cross a cross is that it kills the one who carries it; it puts to death that part of the disciple that God knows must die for salvation to work." These are the words of American scholar and author Fr. Paul Mankowski, SJ. Is a cross from God putting to death what needs to die in you?

"Because [Jesus] himself was tested through what he suffered, he is able to help those who are being tested" (Heb 2:18). Tell Jesus about your worst recent suffering (or a suffering you're currently going through). How do you think he could help you in your trial?

"If you look for the bad in people expecting to find it, you surely will," said Abraham Lincoln. Ask Jesus to show you the good in people, especially difficult people, in your life. What does Jesus say in reply?

G. K. Chesterton stated, "An inconvenience is only an adventure wrongly considered; an adventure is only an inconvenience rightly considered." Can you begin to view an inconvenience in your life as an adventure? Can you be like the hero in a story who confronts (and eventually overcomes) a challenge? Write about an inconvenience in your life.

Saint Paul describes his dramatic conversion: "I fell to the ground and heard a voice saying to me, 'Saul, Saul, why are you persecuting me?' I replied, 'Who are you, sir?' And he said to me, 'I am Jesus the Nazorean whom you are persecuting'" (Acts 22:7–8). Jesus is present in his Church, and that means Jesus is also present in you. How is Jesus present in your suffering now?

After suffering fifteen years of hard labor in a Soviet gulag in Siberia, Fr. Walter J. Ciszek wrote, "The greatest grace God can give [someone] is to send him a trial he cannot bear with his own powers — and then sustain him with his grace so he may endure to the end and be saved." Tell God about your greatest trial. How does God respond?

The great Dominican theologian and Doctor of the Church St. Thomas Aquinas wrote, "Nothing save the love of God can make us love our enemies; for we love them because they are his creatures, made in his image, and capable of enjoying him." Write a letter to God about someone who has treated you as an enemy. What do you think God would say in reply?

We read in the Gospel of Luke: "Some men brought on a stretcher a man who was paralyzed; they were trying to bring him in and set [him] in his presence. But not finding a way to bring him in because of the crowd, they went up on the roof and lowered him" (5:18–19). Who is suffering in your life? How can you bring this person the comfort of Jesus? How does Jesus respond to their suffering? How does he respond to your concern?

In 1531, on Mount Tepeyac in Mexico, Our Lady of Guadalupe appeared to a poor peasant named Juan Diego, saying to him: "Am I not here, I, who am your Mother? Are you not under my shadow and protection? Am I not the source of your joy? Are you not in the hollow of my mantle, in the crossing of my arms? Do you need anything more? Let nothing else worry you, disturb you." Imagine if Mary said these words to you. How would you reply? How would Mary reply to you?

Jesus said to the crowds: "Come to me, all you who labor and are burdened, and I will give you rest. Take my yoke upon you and learn from me, for I am meek and humble of heart; and you will find rest for yourselves. For my yoke is easy, and my burden light" (Mt 11:28–30). Write a letter to Christ about your own greatest burden, and imagine what he says when you give this burden to his merciful care.

The Spanish mystic St. John of the Cross wrote, "Strive to preserve your heart in peace; let no event of this world disturb it." If Jesus wrote to you, how would he recommend that you grow in peace despite the real difficulties of your life? Write back to Jesus about how you might practice these recommendations.

Frederick Buechner, Protestant minister and theologian, wrote: "Of the Seven Deadly Sins, anger is possibly the most fun. To lick your wounds, to smack your lips over grievances long past, to roll over your tongue the prospect of bitter confrontations still to come, to savor to the last toothsome morsel both the pain you are given and the pain you are giving back — in many ways it is a feast fit for a king. The chief drawback is that what you are wolfing down is yourself. The skeleton at the feast is you." Ask Jesus how you can find forgiveness to extinguish sinful anger.

St. Josephine Bakhita was a tortured slave from Sudan who gained her freedom and became a religious sister. Someone once asked her, "What would you do, if you were to meet your captors?" Saint Josephine replied: "If I were to meet those who kidnapped me, and even those who tortured me, I would kneel and kiss their hands. For, if these things had not happened, I would not have been a Christian and a religious today." Has God ever brought good out of something bad happening to you?

Pope Benedict XVI wrote, "You who say in silence 'Jesus, I trust in You' teach us that there is no faith more profound, no hope more alive and no love more ardent than the faith, hope and love of a person who in the midst of suffering places himself securely in God's hands." Write about your difficulties in detail, but keep adding, "Jesus, I trust in you to help with this" or "Jesus, I trust in you to handle that."

"We don't always want our suffering; we are tight-fisted about it, haggle over it, often botch the job. There is suffering that has been done well just as there is work that has been done well," said the Venerable Madeleine Delbrêl, a twentieth-century French Catholic author, poet, and mystic. How can you suffer well today?

Professor Miroslav Volf, founding director of the Yale Center for Faith and Culture, wrote: "Forgiveness flounders because I exclude the enemy from the community of humans even as I exclude myself from the community of sinners. But no one can be in the presence of the God of the crucified Messiah for long without overcoming this double exclusion." Write to Jesus while imagining yourself at the foot of the cross, standing next to whomever it is that you dislike the most.

The Gospel of John records that as Christ was dying on the cross, "When Jesus saw his mother and the disciple there whom he loved, he said to his mother, 'Woman, behold, your son.' Then he said to the disciple, 'Behold, your mother'" (19:26–27). Jesus gave Mary to be the adopted mother of his baptized brothers and sisters in the family of God, including you and me. In your own suffering, as you carry your own cross, Mary is also there with you. Write to Mary about your suffering and imagine what Our Lady of Sorrows might say to you in reply.

In the Gospel of Matthew, it is written: "When Herod realized that he had been deceived by the magi, he became furious. He ordered the massacre of all the boys in Bethlehem and its vicinity two years old and under, in accordance with the time he had ascertained from the magi " (2:16). Do you have a Herod in your life? Is there an angry, vicious person who seems intent on destroying what is innocent and good? Are you sometimes a Herod to yourself? Write to Jesus about your own Herod. What does Jesus say in reply?

Pope Benedict XVI wrote, "If discouragement overwhelms you, think of the faith of Joseph; if anxiety has its grip on you, think of the hope of Joseph; if exasperation or hatred seizes you, think of the love of Joseph, who was the first man to set eyes on the human face of God." If you could ask Saint Joseph to pray to God for a special favor for you, what would it be? If Joseph responded to you, imagine what he'd say.

The Harvard psychiatrist and Catholic Dr. Kevin Majeres holds that addictions are always forms of escaping challenges, escaping suffering. How can you reframe the challenges of your life as opportunities to grow in skills, in virtues, and bonds with others?

Alexander Pope, an eighteenth-century British poet and satirist, said, "No one should be ashamed to admit they are wrong, which is but saying, in other words, that they are wiser today than they were yesterday." Can you admit to God that you have been wrong and caused suffering to yourself and others? Can you admit you were wrong to others you may have hurt?

"My whole strength lies in prayer and sacrifice; these are my invincible arms; they can move hearts far better than words," said St. Thérèse of Lisieux. What beautiful prayer and sacrifice can you offer to God today?

Jesus taught his disciples, "If anyone wishes to come after me, he must deny himself and take up his cross daily and follow me" (Lk 9:23). What small cross can you embrace today to serve the needs of others?

"And Mary said, 'My soul proclaims the greatness of the Lord; my spirit rejoices in God my savior. For he has looked upon his handmaid's lowliness; behold, from now on will all ages call me blessed'" (Lk 1:46–48). Write to Mary asking her to pray to God to make you blessed in your own lowliness so that you too might rejoice in God your savior. How do you think Mary would respond to what you wrote?

Doctor of the Church St. Teresa of Ávila advised: "Let nothing disturb you. Let nothing frighten you. Those who cling to God will lack nothing. God alone is enough." How can God comfort you today in your fears?

In a dream an angel said: "Joseph, son of David, do not be afraid to take Mary your wife into your home. For it is through the holy Spirit that this child has been conceived in her. She will bear a son and you are to name him Jesus, because he will save his people from their sins" (Mt 1:20–21). Joseph overcame his fear on many occasions to serve Jesus and Mary. Do you have fears that hinder you from serving Jesus and Mary? Ask God about your fear and ask him to increase your courage so that you might love despite your fears.

"People are generally the carpenters of their own crosses," said St. Philip Neri, a sixteenth-century Italian priest and founder of the Congregation of the Oratory. Write to God about a time when you were your own worst enemy. How can God help you grow from this experience?

St. John Henry Newman, a nineteenth-century convert from Anglicanism who was made a cardinal, said, "We should ever conduct ourselves towards our enemy as if he were one day to be our friend." Is there an "enemy" in your life whom you can make into a friend?

"In order to arrive at possessing everything, desire to possess nothing," said the Spanish mystic St. John of the Cross. What desires to possess can you give up so that your desires for God increase?

PART III

Discovering God's Will

Everywhere, O Truth Divine, you listen to all who ask you for guidance. You answer all, even though they ask for your guidance on diverse matters. You always answer everyone, but not everyone listens to you. All can ask for your counsel about whatever they want, but not all hear what they want to hear. Your best servants don't always hear what they want to hear, but rather they want whatever they hear from you. Too late loved I You, O Beauty ever ancient and ever new. Too late have I loved You.
CONFESSIONS, BOOK TEN

In his journey of faith, Augustine faced many questions. Some of these were intellectual. How can we make sense of the problem of evil? How should we understand stories from the Old Testament? Can we really come to know the truth? Many more of his questions were existential. What work should I do? Where should I live? What is the best way to live?

Each one of us faces our own questions. We may not always know the next step forward in terms of our work, our relationships, and our lives. When we write to God about our questions, and especially if we repeatedly seek divine Wisdom in finding the answers, we can move forward in confidence that God is guiding us. Ask and you shall receive. Knock and it shall be opened to you. In your own journey, you can make your own these words of St. John Henry Newman:

> Lead, Kindly Light, amidst th'encircling gloom,
> Lead Thou me on!
> The night is dark, and I am far from home,
> Lead Thou me on!
> Keep Thou my feet; I do not ask to see
> The distant scene; one step enough for me.

If you compare yourself to who you were last week, last month, last year, are you moving as guided by the Kindly Light?

Scripture reminds us, "Prepare the way of the Lord, make straight his paths" (Mk 1:3). What would Jesus say to you about the best way to prepare for him? How do you respond?

The Immaculate Conception of Mary is the beginning of the end of evil. No one knew that the daughter of Anne would be the mother of God. But God's grace was preparing Mary, freeing her from original sin from the very beginning of her life, so that she could be the mother of Jesus, and our mother. If you could receive a special grace from God today to make you ready for your personal mission, what would you ask for? What would Jesus or Mary say in reply?

Venerable Fulton Sheen once wrote: "As God was physically formed in Mary, so he wills to be spiritually formed in you. If you knew he was seeing through your eyes, you would see in everyone a child of God. If you knew that he worked through your hands, they would bless all the day through. ... If you knew that he wants to use your mind, your will, your fingers, and your heart, how different you would be." Imagine what God would write to you today to make use of your mind, your body, your will, and your decisions in your everyday life. How can you respond to God's invitation today?

The medieval mystic Thomas à Kempis wrote: "He who assists a brother in need holds Jesus by the hand. He who patiently bears the burdens placed upon him carries Jesus crucified on his shoulders. He who speaks consoling words to a saddened brother gives Jesus a tender kiss. He who regrets another's fault and prays for his pardon washes and wipes Jesus' feet. He who remakes an angry person into one of peace prepares a bed of flowers for Jesus in his soul." Write to Jesus about a person you can help today.

St. John Chrysostom said, "For by gold the power of a king is signified, by frankincense the honor of God, by myrrh the burial of the body; and accordingly they offer him gold as King, frankincense as God, myrrh as Man." What gifts can you bring baby Jesus today? How is God calling you today, in your ordinary life, to give him a gift of your service? Who in your life is vulnerable and needy like a little child?

The English essayist G. K. Chesterton wrote: "Right is right, even if no-body does it. Wrong is wrong, even if everybody is wrong about it." What does Jesus want to teach you about right and wrong? How are you called to live counterculturally?

The poet W. H. Auden wrote, "We would rather be ruined than changed, / We would rather die in dread / Than climb the cross of the moment / And let our illusions die." What illusions keep you from deeper love of God? How could God free you?

"For whoever has scorned such a day of small things will rejoice to see the capstone in the hand of Zerubbabel" (Zec 4:10). Ask God whether he wants you to begin something new for his sake. What does God say in reply?

The French novelist Léon Bloy once wrote, "The only real sadness, the only real failure, the only great tragedy in life, is not to become a saint." Ask Jesus what you would need to do to be a saint. How would he answer you? What would you say in reply?

In his *Confessions*, Augustine said to God, "You gave me the gift of not wanting more than you gave me." How can you seek to want what God wants to give us and what God has already given you — rather than what you happen to want?

In the Gospel of John, we read that Jesus said: "No one has greater love than this, to lay down one's life for one's friends. You are my friends. … I have called you friends, because I have told you everything I have heard from my Father" (15:12–15). Jesus wants to be your best friend. Imagine what he would say to you in a letter inviting you to be best friends. How would you respond?

John the Baptist "came for testimony, to testify to the light, so that all might believe through him" (Jn 1:7). How does Jesus call you to be his witness, and how can you respond?

Each day Pope St. John XXIII had a resolution: "Only for today, I will seek to live the livelong day positively without wishing to solve the problems of my life all at once." What one small problem can you tackle today? What huge problems can you leave for God to take care of himself? Write to Jesus about how to make the resolution of John XXIII a reality.

St. John of the Cross wrote, "Where there is no love, put love — and you will find love." Who needs your love, especially today?

In the Old Testament, God teaches his chosen people, "See, I have today set before you life and good, death and evil. I have set before you life and death, the blessing and the curse. Choose life, then, that you and your descendants may live" (Dt 30:15,19). Write to Jesus about how you can promote a culture of life, and imagine what Jesus says in reply.

Jesus said: "Let your 'Yes' mean 'Yes,' and your 'No,' 'No.' Anything more is from the evil one" (Mt 5:37). How can you be more honest and truthful?

Fr. Bernard Lonergan, SJ, a Canadian philosopher and theologian, advised, "Be attentive, be intelligent, be responsible, be loving, and, if necessary, change." Do you think change is necessary in your life? What do you imagine God has to say to you about that — and how will he help you make any needed changes?

"Don't wait until everything is just right. There will always be challenges, obstacles, and less than perfect conditions. So what. Get started now. With each step you take, you will grow stronger and stronger," wrote the author and speaker Mark Victor Hansen. Ask the Lord what you can do today to take a step in the right direction. How does he respond?

EWTN founder Mother Angelica wrote, "God from all eternity chose you to be where you are, at this time in history, to change the world." How could you, with God's help, change your corner of the world for the better today?

St. John Henry Newman wrote a hymn that begins, "Lead, Kindly Light, amidst th'encircling gloom, / Lead Thou me on! / The night is dark, and I am far from home, / Lead Thou me on! Keep Thou my feet; I do not ask to see / The distant scene; one step enough for me." How do you experience Christ as the light in the darkness? Where is [his] Kindly Light leading you, and is anything holding you back from following?

The Notre Dame theologian Fr. Brian Daley, SJ, once wrote these words to a young man whom he served as a spiritual director. The young man was questioning whether he had properly discerned God's will in his vocation. Fr. Daley wrote: "'If your child asks you for bread, would you give him a stone? If he asks for fish, would you give him a scorpion?' And if we, who are evil, would never do this to our child, would God who is all good do it to us? After we have asked so earnestly for light and guidance, would he let you make a disastrous decision? Would he deceive you into thinking something was his will and his gift, when it was really a destructive choice? We simply can't ascribe that kind of malevolence to God!" What is God's will for you? Are you discerning a path forward? Can you trust in God that he has guided you already?

Saint Polycarp, a disciple of St. John the Apostle and an early Christian martyr, said, "Hear me declare with boldness, I am a Christian." Ask God how you can declare your faith and love of Christ today in what you say and what you do.

After giving away her vast fortune to help those in need, St. Katharine Drexel said, "If we wish to serve God and love our neighbor well, we must manifest our joy in the service we render to him and them." How can you become a more cheerful giver to those who need or want your help?

Civil rights leader Rev. Dr. Martin Luther King Jr. said, "The time is always right to do right." Is there anything that you know is right to do that you have put off doing? Can you, with God's help, do it today?

Saint Paul teaches: "And the Lord's servant must not be quarrelsome but kindly to every one, an apt teacher, forbearing, correcting his opponents with gentleness. God may perhaps grant that they will repent and come to know the truth" (2 Tm 2:24–25, RSV). How can you become a better servant of the Lord?

The Jesuit missionary St. Francis Xavier traveled across the globe with courage and haste to spread the Gospel. He said, "Many, many people hereabouts are not becoming Christians for one reason only: there is nobody to make them Christians." Ask Jesus how you can evangelize today in your own time and place among your friends and acquaintances. How can you share the good news of what God has done for you? What does Jesus say in reply to your testimony?

In his *Confessions*, Augustine wrote, "Here's the ground on which a weak soul lies, not yet clinging to truth's solidity: whatever breezes blow, delivered by human tongues out of the bosom of humanity's various views, they can carry that soul around and about, twist it inside out, while the light is clouded over and the truth not perceived — but it's right in front of us." How can you more firmly ground yourself in God's truth, rather than the passing fashions of various human views?

When the Angel Gabriel announced to Mary that she would be the mother of Jesus, Mary said, "Behold, I am the handmaid of the Lord. May it be done to me according to your word" (Lk 1:38). Write about how you can embrace God's mysterious will and say to God with Mary, "May it be done to me according to your word."

Timothy Keller, an American Protestant pastor, theologian, and best-selling author, said: "Think of how God won you over. Not by taking power but by coming and losing power and serving you. How did God save you? He came not with a sword in his hand but with nails in his hands. He came not to bring judgment but to bear judgment." How can you win others for God by your love and mercy?

St. Josemaría Escrivá once wrote: "Don't let your life be barren. Be useful. Make yourself felt. Shine forth with the torch of your faith and your love." How could you be useful to those in your life today? If you wrote to God about this, what do you think God would say back?

In his *Confessions*, Augustine recounts his mother Monica's warning to him to avoid sin. He writes: "They were *your* warnings, and I didn't know. I thought you were silent, and she was speaking, though it was through her that you *weren't* silent." Is God's voice speaking to you through someone in your life? Can you hear the divine call spoken through a human voice?

St. John Neumann, the fourth bishop of Philadelphia, wrote: "Everyone who breathes, high and low, educated and ignorant, young and old, man and woman, has a mission, has a work. We are not sent into this world for nothing; we are not born at random." For what purpose did God make you? What further purposes does God have for you?

Venerable Fulton Sheen said: "We always make the fatal mistake of thinking that it is what we do that matters, when really what matters is what we let God do to us. God sent the angel to Mary, not to ask her to do something, but to let something be done. Since God is a better artisan than you, the more you abandon yourself to him, the happier he can make you." What can you let God do with you? How does God respond?

"About the only way we know whether we believe or not is by what we do," said Flannery O'Connor. What can you do today to manifest your belief?

Conclusion

You can go back and review what you have written. What patterns or themes emerge and capture your attention? Write about them in a final letter below. Thank God for speaking to you through these letters. If you would like to continue praying like Saint Augustine, consider picking up a copy of Saint Augustine's *Confessions*. (I'd recommend Sarah Ruden's translation.) Each time a line jumps out at you, you can use it as a point of reflection to write your own letter to God.

For future letters, you might also try reading through the Gospel portion read at Mass. Then read it again slowly, and imagine what Jesus is saying to you right now through this reading. You can then write a response to Jesus.

About the Author

Dr. Christopher Kaczor is Chair of the Department of Philosophy at Loyola Marymount University and Professor for the Renewal of Catholic Intellectual Life at Bishop Barron's Word on Fire Institute. He graduated from the Honors Program of Boston College and earned a Ph.D. four years later from the University of Notre Dame studying under the legendary Ralph McInerny. A Fulbright Scholar, Dr. Kaczor did postdoctoral work as an Alexander von Humboldt German Chancellor Fellow at the University of Cologne. He was appointed a Corresponding Member of the Pontifical Academy for Life and William E. Simon Visiting Fellow in the James Madison Program at Princeton University. The winner of a Templeton Grant, he has written more than 100 scholarly articles and book chapters. An award winning author, his sixteen books include *Disputes in Bioethics*, *Thomas Aquinas on the Cardinal Virtues*, *365 Days to Deeper Faith*, *The Gospel of Happiness*, *The Seven Big Myths about Marriage*, *A Defense of Dignity*, and *The Seven Big Myths about the Catholic Church*. Dr. Kaczor's views have been in *The New York Times*, *Newsweek*, the *Washington Post*, the *Wall Street Journal*, the *Los Angeles Times*, the *Huffington Post*, *National Review*, NPR, BBC, EWTN, ABC, NBC, FOX, CBS, MSNBC, TEDx, and the *TODAY Show*.

You might also like:

Fathers of the Faith: Saint Augustine
By Mike Aquilina

In this volume from the *Fathers of the Faith* series, you'll be introduced to Saint Augustine of Hippo. Who was he? What did he teach? Where and when did he live? Why is he an important figure in the history of the Church?

In this accessible, bite-sized introduction, renowned author, speaker, and television host Mike Aquilina gives an overview of Augustine's life as a proud North African in the fourth and fifth century. His conversion from sinful young man to Catholic priest and bishop is well known from his autobiography, *Confessions*.

One of the four great Doctors of the Church, Augustine is considered the authority on almost everything because he wrote about practically everything. He incorporated the best of secular philosophy and science into his thought. His works are an encyclopedia of the Christian faith, and his writings have impacted countless millions.

Available at
OSVCatholicBookstore.com
or wherever books are sold

You might also like:

Confessions (Noll Library)
By Augustine of Hippo

In *Confessions*, Augustine tells the story of his sinful youth and conversion to Christianity. He describes his ascent from a humble farm in North Africa to a prestigious post in Milan, his struggle against his own sexuality, his renunciation of secular ambition and marriage, and the recovery of his faith. Augustine's concerns are often strikingly contemporary, and the confessional mode he invented can be seen in writings today.